The Biblical Message of Healing

The Reverend Canon
Carl G. Carlozzi, D. Min.

CHURCH HYMNAL CORPORATION, NEW YORK

Scripture verses are taken from *The Living Bible* © 1971. Used by
permission of Tyndale House Publishers, Inc., Wheaton, IL 60189.
All rights reserved.

The Church Hymnal Corporation
800 Second Avenue, New York, NY 10017

5 4 3 2 1

In Thanksgiving for
The Wonderful Staff, Parishioners, Parents
and Students of
All Saints' Church and Day School
Phoenix, Arizona

To The Reader

For purposes of clarity of understanding, all passages of scripture in this book are taken from The Living Bible, Tyndale House Publishers, Wheaton, Illinois, and are used with permission.

$\mathscr{C}$ONTENTS

chapter two

chapter four

chapter five

Introduction

God's desire is for you to be as healthy and whole in mind, body and spirit as life's practical realities will allow. Mercy and healing are our heavenly Father's nature. The psalmist declared God's glory and his wonderful promises of healing:

> I bless the holy name of God with all my heart. Yes, I will bless the Lord and not forget the glorious things he does for me. He forgives all my sins. He heals me. He ransoms me from hell. He surrounds me with loving kindness and tender mercies. He fills my life with good things! My youth is renewed like the eagle's! (Psalm 103:1-5)

The Bible is full of God's promises to us—promises to forgive our sins, to heal us, and to give us abundant life. All these promises have their fulfillment in Jesus Christ who came to die for our sins and rose again that we might have eternal life. Indeed, the ultimate healing for all of us comes when we are called home to be with God in Heaven.

1

While he was on earth, however, Jesus healed many who were ill and afflicted, forgiving their sins and freeing them from their pain and distress. Jesus also gave authority and power to his disciples and to all those who believe in him to heal the sick and the afflicted in his name. This power is at work today among his followers and you and I deny ourselves the full potentiality of God's intent for us while we live on earth if we do not take full advantage of all the spiritual, medical and psychological resources available to supplement our Bible study and prayers.

This book gathers together all of God's promises concerning healing. It is the wise and prudent person who will claim these promises of God, offer their prayers of faith, and then take action by availing themselves of the appropriate avenues of healing which God both blesses and provides: (a) priestly laying-on-of hands; (b) medical and/or surgical treatment; and (c) psychological counseling and therapy.

Chapter One of this book presents God's promises and purposes for your healing. Section I lists the many promises God gives concerning healing and abundant life. Section II contains guidelines for your response to God's promises.

Chapter Two contains prayers based on Scripture. These may be helpful to you as you pray about your illness and ask God for his healing in your life.

2

Chapter Three contains biblical accounts of the healing miracles which Jesus Christ performed while he was on earth. Following this are the accounts of the healings which Jesus' disciples performed and Jesus' promises of authority and healing power to those who believe in him. Hopefully, these biblical accounts of healing will encourage you and reassure you of God's desire to bring healing into your life.

Although this book lists specific verses from the Bible, it is important to read the Scriptures in their context. Use this book as a reference, and when a promise or an account of God's healing is personally meaningful, look up the passage in your Bible and read the verses before and after the passage to better understand God's Word.

Chapter Four offers practical suggestions and encouragement. Use these varied prayers during the many stages of your life and healing process.

Chapter Five provides an opportunity for you to keep your own personal journey of healing, including notes, prayers, and experiences.

May God's peace and blessing be with you!

Carl G. Carlozzi
Phoenix, Arizona
Feast of the Transfiguration, 1992

CHAPTER ONE

God's Healing In My Life

Key Verse:

Is anyone among you suffering? He should keep on praying about it. And those who have reason to be thankful should continually be singing praises to the Lord. Is anyone sick? He should call for the elders of the church and they should pray over him and pour a little oil upon him, calling on the Lord to heal him. And their prayer, if offered in faith, will heal him, for the Lord will make him well; and if his sickness was caused by some sin, the Lord will forgive him.   James 5:13-15

God's Promises Of Healing For Me

God promises to heal his people

1. I will give you back your health again and heal your wounds. Jeremiah 30:17

2. If you do these things, God will shed his own glorious light upon you. He will heal you; your godliness will lead you forward, and goodness will be a shield before you and the glory of the Lord will protect you from behind. Isaiah 58:8

3. Peace, peace to them, both near and far, for I will heal them all. Isaiah 57:19

4. I bless the holy name of God with all my heart. Yes, I will bless the Lord and not forget the glorious things he does for me. He forgives all my sins. He heals me. He ransoms me from hell. He surrounds me with loving-kindness and tender mercies. He fills my life with good

things! My youth is renewed like the eagle's!
Psalm 103:1-5

5. He feels pity for the weak and needy, and will rescue them. Psalm 73:13

6. What a glorious Lord! He who daily bears our burdens also gives us our salvation. He frees us! He rescues us from death.   Psalm 68:19-20

7. I have seen what they do, but I will heal them anyway! Isaiah 57:18

8. For Jehovah hears the cries of his needy ones, and does not look the other way. Psalm 69:33

9. I myself will be the Shepherd of my sheep, and cause them to lie down in peace, the Lord God says. I will seek my lost ones, those who strayed away, and bring them safely home again. I will put splints and bandages upon their broken limbs and heal the sick. Ezekiel 34:15-16

10. You can get anything—anything you ask for in prayer—if you believe. Matthew 21:22

11. I also tell you this—if two of you agree down here on earth concerning anything you ask for, my Father in heaven will do it for you. For where two or three gather together because they are mine, I will be right there among them. Matthew 18:19-20

1. He personally carried the load of our sins in his own body when he died on the cross, so that we can be finished with sin and live a good life from now on. For his wounds have healed ours! 1 Peter 2:24

2. The Spirit of the Lord is upon me; he has appointed me to preach Good News to the poor; he has sent me to heal the broken-hearted and to announce that captives shall be released and the blind shall see, that the downtrodden shall be freed from their oppressors, and that God is ready to give blessings to all who come to him. Luke 4:18-19

3. But he was wounded and bruised for our sins. He was chastised that we might have peace; he was lashed—and we were healed! Isaiah 53:5

4. He took our sicknesses and bore our diseases. Matthew 8:17b

5. Sick people need the doctor, not healthy ones! I haven't come to tell good people to repent, but the bad ones. Mark 3:17b

6. How earnestly I tell you this—anyone who believes in me already has eternal life! Yes, I am the Bread of Life!...I am that Living Bread that came down out of heaven. Anyone eating this

Bread shall live forever; this bread is my flesh given to redeem humanity. John 6:47, 48, 51

7. So Jesus said it again, "With all the earnestness I possess I tell you this: Unless you eat the flesh of the Messiah and drink his blood, you cannot have eternal life within you. But anyone who does eat my flesh and drink my blood has eternal life, and I will raise him at the Last Day. For my flesh is the true food, and my blood is the true drink. Everyone who eats my flesh and drinks my blood is in me, and I in him. I live by the power of the living Father who sent me, and in the same way those who partake of me shall live because of me!...anyone who eats this Bread shall live forever." John 6:53-57, 58b

God heals those who are faithful and trust in him

1. For you bless the godly man, O Lord; you protect him with your shield of love. Psalm 5:12

2. The Lord saves the godly! He is their salvation and their refuge when trouble comes. Psalm 37:39

3. This poor man cried to the Lord—and the Lord heard him and saved him out of his troubles. Psalm 34:6

4. I ask you again, does God give you the power

of the Holy Spirit and work miracles among you as a result of your trying to obey the Jewish laws? No, of course not. It is when you believe in Christ and fully trust him. Galatians 3:5

Although I am afraid and discouraged, God promises to heal me

1. Because the Lord is my Shepherd, I have everything I need! He lets me rest in the meadow grass and leads me beside the quiet streams. He restores my failing health. He helps me do what honors him the most. Even when walking through the dark valley of death I will not be afraid, for you are close beside me, guarding, guiding all the way. You provide delicious food for me in the presence of my enemies. You have welcomed me as your guest; blessings overflow! Your goodness and unfailing kindness shall be with me all of my life, and afterwards I will live with you forever in your home. Psalm 23

2. God is our refuge and strength, a tested help in times of trouble. And so we need not fear even if the world blows up, and the mountains crumble into the sea. Psalm 46:1-2

3. O my soul, why be so gloomy and discouraged?

Trust in God! I shall again praise him for his wondrous help; he will make me smile again, for he is my God! Psalm 43:5

4. The Lord is my light and my salvation; whom shall I fear? Psalm 27:1

5. Then, Lord, you turned your face away from me and cut off your river of blessings. Suddenly my courage was gone; I was terrified and panic-stricken, I cried to you, O Lord; oh, how I pled: Hear me, Lord; oh, have pity and help me. Then he turned my sorrow into joy! He took away my clothes of mourning and gave me gay and festive garments to rejoice in so that I might sing glad praises to the Lord instead of lying in silence in the grave. O Lord my God, I will keep on thanking you forever! Psalm 30:7b-8, 10-12

6. As the deer pants for water, so I long for you, O God. I thirst for God, the living God. Where can I find him to come and stand before him? Take courage, my soul! Do you remember those times (but how could you ever forget them!) when you led a great procession to the Temple on festival days, singing with joy, praising the Lord? Why then be downcast? Why be discouraged and sad? Hope in God! I shall yet

praise him again. Yes, I shall again praise him for his help. Psalm 42:1-2, 4-5

Even in my weakness, I can depend on God and his strength

1. Each time he said, "No. But I am with you; that is all you need. My power shows up best in weak people." Now I am glad to boast about how weak I am; I am glad to be a living demonstration of Christ's power, instead of showing off my own power and abilities. Since I know it is all for Christ's good, I am quite happy about "the thorn," and about insults and hardships, persecutions and difficulties; for when I am weak, then I am strong—the less I have, the more I depend on him. 2 Corinthians 12:9-10

2. For to you has been given the privilege not only of trusting him but also of suffering for him. Philippians 1:29

3. If you are filled with light within, with no dark corners, then your face will be radiant too, as though a floodlight is beamed upon you. Luke 11:36

Even if I feel God has deserted me, he still promises to heal me

1. Blessed is the Lord, for he has shown me that his never-failing love protects me like the walls of a fort! I spoke too hastily when I said, "The Lord has deserted me," for you listened to my plea and answered me. Psalm 31:21-22

2. "O God my Rock," I cry, "why have you forsaken me? Why must I suffer these attacks from my enemies?" Their taunts pierce me like a fatal wound; again and again they scoff, "Where is that God of yours?" But O my soul, don't be discouraged. Don't be upset. Expect God to act! For I know that I shall again have plenty of reason to praise him for all that he will do. He is my help! He is my God! Psalm 42:9-11

3. Lord, when doubts fill my mind, when my heart is in turmoil, quiet me and give me renewed hope and cheer. Psalm 94:19

4. I waited patiently for God to help me; then he listened and heard my cry. He lifted me out of the pit of despair, out from the bog and the mire, and set my feet on a hard, firm path and steadied me as I walked along. He has given me a new song to sing, of praises to our God.

Now many will hear of the glorious things he did for me, and stand in awe before the Lord, and put their trust in him. Psalm 40:1-3

God's promise of the resurrection

1. Jesus told her, "I am the one who raises the dead and gives them life again. Anyone who believes in me, even though he dies like anyone else, shall live again. He is given eternal life for believing in me and shall never perish." John 11:25-26a

2. But as for me, I know that my Redeemer lives, and that he will stand upon the earth at last. And I know that after this body has decayed, this body shall see God! Then he will be on my side! Yes, I shall see him, not as a stranger, but as a friend! What a glorious hope! Job 19:25-27

3. Yet, even though Christ lives within you, your body will die because of sin; but your spirit will live, for Christ has pardoned it. And if the Spirit of God, who raised up Jesus from the dead, lives in you, he will make your dying bodies live again after you die, by means of this same Holy Spirit living within you. Romans 8:10-11

4. And since we are his children, we will share his treasures—for all God gives to his Son Jesus is now ours too. But if we are to share his glory,

we must also share his suffering. Yet what we suffer now is nothing compared to the glory he will give us later. Romans 8:17-18

5. For we know that even the things of nature, like animals and plants, suffer in sickness and death as they await this great event. And even we Christians, although we have the Holy Spirit within us as a foretaste of future glory, also groan to be released from pain and suffering. We, too, wait anxiously for that day when God will give us our full rights as his children, including the new bodies he has promised us— bodies that will never be sick again and will never die. Romans 8:22-23

6. For the Scriptures tell us that no one who believes in Christ will ever be disappointed. Romans 10:11

7. In the same way, our earthly bodies which die and decay are different from the bodies we shall have when we come back to life again, for they will never die. The bodies we have now embarrass us for they become sick and die; but they will be full of glory when we come back to life again. Yes, they are weak, dying bodies now, but when we live again they will be full of strength. They are just human bodies at death, but when they come back to life they will be superhuman bodies. For just as there are natural, human bodies, there are also supernatural, spiritual bodies. 1 Corinthians 15:42-44

8. When this happens, then at last this Scripture will come true—"Death is swallowed up in victory." O death, where then your victory? Where then your sting? For sin—the sting that causes death—will all be gone; and the law, which reveals our sins, will no longer be our judge. How we thank God for all of this! It is he who makes us victorious through Jesus Christ our Lord! 1 Corinthians 15:54-57

9. So, my dear brothers, since future victory is sure, be strong and steady, always abounding in the Lord's work, for you know that nothing you do for the Lord is ever wasted as it would be if there were no resurrection. 1 Corinthians 15:58

My Response To God's Promises Of Healing

I can help promote God's healing in my life

1. Be delighted with the Lord. Then he will give you all your heart's desires. Commit everything you do to the Lord. Trust him to help you do it and he will. Psalm 37:4-5

2. But for you who fear my name, the Sun of Righteousness will rise with healing in his wings. Malachi 4:2a

3. But the eyes of the Lord are watching over those who fear him, who rely upon his steady love. He will keep them from death even in times of famine! We depend upon the Lord alone to save us. Only he can help us; he protects us like a shield. Psalm 33:18-20

4. God blesses those who are kind to the poor. He helps them out of their troubles. He protects them and keeps them alive; he publicly honors them and destroys the power of their enemies. He nurses them when they are sick, and soothes their pains and worries. Psalm 41:1-3

5. Come, let us return to the Lord; it is he who has torn us—he will heal us. He has wounded—he will bind us up. Hosea 6:1

6. If you belong to the Lord, reverence him; for everyone who does this has everything he needs. Psalm 34:9

7. For the Angel of the Lord guards and rescues all who reverence him. Psalm 34:7

8. But I will rejoice in the Lord. He shall rescue me! Psalm 35:9

9. Carry out my instructions; don't forget them, for they will lead you to real living. Proverbs 4:13

10. Don't be conceited, sure of your own wisdom. Instead, trust and reverence the Lord, and turn your back on evil; when you do that, then you will be given renewed health and vitality. Proverbs 3:7-8

11. Stop your anger! Turn off your wrath. Don't fret and worry—it only leads to harm. Psalm 37:8

I can open the channels of healing by meditating on and obeying God's Word

1. Lord, see how much I really love your demands. Now give me back my life and health because you are so kind. Psalm 119:159

2. I am completely discouraged—I lie in the dust. Revive me by your Word. I told you my plans and you replied. Now give me your instructions. Make me understand what you want; for then I shall see your miracles. Psalm 119:25-27

3. If you will listen to the voice of the Lord your God, and obey it, and do what is right, then I will not make you suffer the diseases I send on the Egyptians, for I am the Lord who heals you. Exodus 15:26

4. You shall serve the Lord our God only; then I will bless you with food and water, and I will take away sickness from among you. Exodus 23:25

5. God is my shield; he will defend me. He saves those whose hearts and lives are true and right. Psalm 7:10

6. Listen, son of mine, to what I say. Listen carefully. Keep these thoughts ever in mind; let them penetrate deep within your heart, for

they will mean real life for you, and radiant health. Proverbs 4:20-22

I can receive God's healing by confessing my sins

1. There was a time when I wouldn't admit what a sinner I was. But my dishonesty made me miserable and filled my days with frustration. All day and all night your hand was heavy on me. My strength evaporated like water on a sunny day until I finally admitted all my sins to you and stopped trying to hide them. I said to myself, "I will confess them to the Lord." And you forgave me! All my guilt is gone. Psalm 32:3-5

2. The Lord is close to those whose hearts are breaking; he rescues those who are humbly sorry for their sins. The good man does not escape all troubles—he has them too. But the Lord helps him in each and every one. Psalm 34:18-19

3. "O Lord," I prayed, "be kind and heal me, for I have confessed my sins." But my enemies say, "May he soon die and be forgotten! It is fatal, whatever it is," they say. "He'll never get out of that bed!" Lord, don't you desert me! Be gracious, Lord, and make me well again so I can

pay them back! I know you are pleased with me because you haven't let my enemies triumph over me. You have preserved me because I was honest; you have admitted me forever to your presence. Psalm 41:4-5, 8, 10-12

My patience can bring God's healing

1. Dear brothers, is your life full of difficulties and temptations? Then be happy, for when the way is rough, your patience has a chance to grow. So let it grow, and don't try to squirm out of your problems. For when your patience is finally in full bloom, then you will be ready for anything, strong in character, full and complete. James 1:2-4

2. Don't be impatient for the Lord to act! Keep traveling steadily along his pathway and in due season he will honor you with every blessing. Psalm 37:34a

3. Don't be impatient. Wait for the Lord, and he will come and save you! Be brave, stouthearted and courageous. Yes, wait and he will help you. Psalm 27:14

4. But they that wait upon the Lord shall renew their strength. They shall mount up with wings

like eagles; they shall run and not be weary; they shall walk and not faint. Isaiah 40:31

5. Keep your eyes on Jesus, our leader and instructor. He was willing to die a shameful death on the cross because of the joy he knew would be his afterwards; and now he sits in the place of honor by the throne of God. If you want to keep from becoming fainthearted and weary, think about his patience as sinful men did such terrible things to him. Hebrews 12:2-3

I must pray in faith for healing

1. What is faith? It is the confident assurance that something we want is going to happen. It is the certainty that what we hope for is waiting for us, even though we cannot see it up ahead. Hebrews 11:1

2. You haven't tried this before, [but begin now]. Ask, using my name, and you will receive, and your cup of joy will overflow. John 16:24

3. If you don't ask with faith, don't expect the Lord to give you any solid answer. James 1:8

4. "If your faith were only the size of a mustard seed," Jesus answered, "it would be large enough to uproot that mulberry tree over there and send

it hurtling into the sea! Your command would bring immediate results! Luke 17:6

5. Oh, praise the Lord, for he has listened to my pleadings! He is my strength, my shield from every danger. I trusted in him, and he helped me. Joy rises in my heart until I burst out in songs of praise to him. Psalm 28:6-7

6. O Lord my God, I pleaded with you, and you gave me my health again. You brought me back from the brink of the grave, from death itself, and here I am alive! Psalm 30:2-3

My spiritual actions can prevent my healing or jeopardize my health

So if anyone eats this bread and drinks from this cup of the Lord in an unworthy manner, he is guilty of sin against the body and the blood of the Lord. That is why a man should examine himself carefully before eating the bread and drinking from the cup. For if he eats the bread and drinks from the cup unworthily, not thinking about the body of Christ and what it means, he is eating and drinking God's judgement upon himself; for he is trifling with the death of Christ. That is why many of you are weak and sick, and some have even died. 1 Corinthians 11:27-30

More ways I can respond to God's promises

1. Some people like to make cutting remarks, but the words of the wise soothe and heal. Proverbs 12:18

2. Kind words are like honey—enjoyable and healthful. Proverbs 16:24

CHAPTER TWO

Prayers for Healing from The Bible

Key Verse:
I reach out for you. I thirst for you as parched land thirsts for rain. Come quickly, Lord, and answer me, for my depression deepens; don't turn away from me or I shall die. Let me see your kindness to me in the morning, for I am trusting you. Show me where to walk, for my prayer is sincere.
Psalm 143:6-8

Personal Prayers For My Healing

When I am afraid

1. Hear the cry of your beloved child—come with mighty power and rescue me. Psalm 108:6

2. To you, O Lord, I pray. Don't fail me, Lord, for I am trusting you. Don't let my enemies succeed. Don't give them victory over me. Psalm 25:1-2

3. O God, have pity, for I am trusting you! I will hide beneath the shadow of your wings until this storm is past. I will cry to the God of heaven who does such wonders for me. He will send down help from heaven to save me, because of his love and his faithfulness. He will rescue me from these liars who are so intent upon destroying me. Psalm 57:1-3

4. May God bless you richly and grant you increasing freedom from all anxiety and fear. 1 Peter 1:2b

5. If you love me, obey me; and I will ask the Father and he will give you another Comforter, and he will never leave you. I am leaving you with a gift—peace of mind and heart! And the peace I give isn't fragile like the peace the world gives. So don't be troubled or afraid. John 14:15-16, 27

When I am discouraged and depressed

1. Hear my prayer, O Lord; listen to my cry! Don't sit back, unmindful of my tears. For I am your guest. I am a traveler passing through the earth as all my fathers were. Spare me, Lord! Let me recover and be filled with happiness again before my death. Psalm 39:12-13

2. O God, you have declared me perfect in your eyes; you have always cared for me in my distress; now hear me as I call again. Have mercy on me. Hear my prayer. Psalm 4:1

3. Save me, O my God. The floods have risen. Deeper and deeper I sink in the mire; the waters rise around me. I have wept until I am exhausted; my throat is dry and hoarse; my eyes are swollen with weeping, waiting for my God to act. But I keep right on praying to you, Lord. For now is the time—you are bending down to hear! You are ready with a plentiful supply of love and kindness. Now answer my prayer and rescue me as you promised. Pull me out of this mire. Don't let me sink in. Rescue me from those who hate me, and from these deep waters I am in. O Jehovah, answer my prayer, for your loving-kindness is wonderful; your mercy is so plentiful, so tender and so kind. Don't hide from me, for I am in deep trouble. Quick! Come and save me. Come, Lord and rescue me. Psalm 69:1-3, 13-14, 16-18a

4. Come, Lord, and show me your mercy, for I am helpless, overwhelmed, in deep distress; my problems go from bad to worse. Oh, save me from them all! See my sorrows; feel my pain; forgive my sins. Psalm 25:16-18

5. O Lord, from the depths of despair I cry for your help: "Hear me! Answer! Help me!" Psalm 130:1-2

6. Hear my prayer, O Lord; answer my plea, because you are faithful to your promises. Don't bring me to trial! For as compared with you, no one is perfect. My enemies chased and caught me. They have knocked me to the ground. They force me to live in the darkness like those in the grave. I am losing all hope; I am paralyzed with fear. Psalm 143:1-4

7. May God our Father and the Lord Jesus Christ give you all of his blessings, and great peace of heart and mind. 1 Corinthians 1:3

When I am weak

1. But I am in deep trouble. Rush to my aid, for only you can help and save me. O Lord, don't delay. Psalm 70:5

2. Oh, do not hide yourself when I am trying to find you. Do not angrily reject your servant. You have been my help in all my trials before; don't leave me now. Don't forsake me, O God of my salvation. Psalm 27:9

3. I stand silently before the Lord, waiting for him to rescue me. For salvation comes from him alone. Yes, he alone is my Rock, my rescuer, defense and fortress. Why then should I be tense with fear when troubles come? Psalm 62:1-2

4. Lord, you are my refuge! Don't let me down! Save me from my enemies, for you are just! Rescue me! Bend down your ear and listen to my plea and save me. Be to me a great protecting Rock, where I am always welcome, safe from all attacks. For you have issued the order to save me. Psalm 71:1-3

5. Lord, you promised to let me live! Never let it be said that God failed me. Psalm 119:116

6. We are praying, too, that you will be filled with his mighty, glorious strength so that you can keep going no matter what happens—always full of the joy of the Lord. Colossians 1:11

When I feel God has deserted me

1. O Lord, don't stay away. O God my Strength, hurry to my aid. Psalm 22:19

2. Bend down and hear my prayer, O Lord, and answer me, for I am deep in trouble. Psalm 86:1

3. Listen closely to my prayer, O God. Hear my urgent cry. I will call to you whenever trouble strikes and you will help me. Psalm 86:6-7

4. And now, in my old age, don't set me aside. Don't forsake me now when my strength is failing. O God, don't stay away! Come quickly! Help! I will keep on expecting you to help me. I praise you more and more. I cannot count the times when you have faithfully rescued me from danger. I will tell everyone how good you are, and of your constant, daily care. I walk in the strength of the Lord God. I tell everyone that you alone are just and good. O God, you have helped me from my earliest childhood—

and I have constantly testified to others of the wonderful things you do. And now that I am old and gray, don't forsake me. Give me time to tell this new generation (and their children too) about all your mighty miracles. Your power and goodness, Lord, reach to the highest heavens. You have done such wonderful things. Where is there another God like you? You have let me sink down deep in desperate problems. But you will bring me back to life again, up from the depths of the earth. You will give me greater honor than before, and turn again and comfort me. Psalm 71:9, 12, 14-21

When I am in pain

1. Pity me, O Lord, for I am weak. Heal me, for my body is sick, and I am upset and disturbed. My mind is filled with apprehension and with gloom. Oh, restore me soon. Psalm 6:2-3

2. Listen to my prayer, O God; don't hide yourself when I cry to you. Hear me, Lord! Listen to me! For I groan and weep beneath any burden of woe. Psalm 55:1-2

As I seek God in faith and trust

1. Lord, you alone can heal me, you alone can

save, and my praises are for you alone. Jeremiah 17:14

2. I plead with you to help me, Lord, for you are my Rock of safety. If you refuse to answer me, I might as well give up and die. Lord, I lift my hands to heaven and implore your help. Oh, listen to my cry. Psalm 28:1-2

3. Lord, how you have helped me before! You took me safely from my mother's womb and brought me through the years of infancy. I have depended upon you since birth; you have always been my God. Don't leave me now, for trouble is near and no one else can possibly help. Psalm 22:9-11

4. Save me, O God, because I have come to you for refuge. I said to him, "You are my Lord; I have no other help but yours." Psalm 16:1-2

5. Protect me as you would the pupil of your eye; hide me in the shadow of your wings as you hover over me. Psalm 17:8

6. You are my refuge and my shield, and your promises are my only source of hope. Psalm 119:114

7. So I pray for you Gentiles that God who gives you hope will keep you happy and full of peace as you believe in him. I pray that God will help

you overflow with hope in him through the Holy Spirit's power within you. Romans 15:13

As I meditate on God's Word

1. I am praying with great earnestness; answer me, O Lord, and I will obey your laws. "Save me," I cry, "for I am obeying." Early in the morning, before the sun is up, I was praying and pointing out how much I trust in you. I stay awake through the night to think about your promises. Because you are so loving and kind, listen to me and make me well again. Psalm 119:145-149

2. O Lord, listen to my prayers; give me the common sense you promised. Hear my prayer; rescue me as you said you would. Psalm 119:169-170

3. Lord, saving me will bring glory to your name. Bring me out of all this trouble because you are true to your promises. Psalm 143:11

As I confess my sins

O Lord, don't hold back your tender mercies from me! My only hope is in your love and faithfulness. Otherwise I perish, for problems far too big for me to solve are piled higher than my head.

Meanwhile my sins, too many to count, have all caught up with me and I am ashamed to look up. My heart quails within me. Please, Lord, rescue me! Quick! Come and help me! Psalm 40:11-13

As I wait patiently for God's answer

1. Come with great power, O God, and save me! Defend me with your might! Oh, listen to my prayer. Psalm 54:1-2

2. Listen to my pleading, Lord! Be merciful and send the help I need. Psalm 27:7

3. O Lord, hear me praying; listen to my plea, O God my King, for I will never pray to anyone but you. Each morning I will look to you in heaven and lay my requests before you, praying earnestly. Psalm 5:1-3

4. How long will you forget me, Lord? Forever? How long will you look the other way when I am in need? How long must I be hiding daily anguish in my heart? How long shall my enemy have the upper hand? Answer me, O Lord my God; give me light in my darkness lest I die. But I will always trust in you and in your mercy and shall rejoice in your salvation. I will sing to the Lord because he has blessed me so richly. Psalm 13:1-3, 5-6

5. Rescue me, O God! Lord, hurry to my aid! Psalm 70:1

When I am facing death

1. O Jehovah, God of my salvation, I have wept before you day and night. Now hear my prayers; oh, listen to my cry, for my life is full of troubles, and death draws near. They say my life is ebbing out—a hopeless case. They have left me here to die, like those slain on battle-fields, from whom your mercies are removed. You have thrust me down to the darkest depths. Your wrath lies heavy on me; wave after wave engulfs me. You have made my friends to loathe me, and they have gone away. I am in a trap with no way out. My eyes grow dim with weeping. Each day I beg your help; O Lord, I reach my pleading hands to you for mercy. Soon it will be too late! Of what use are your miracles when I am in the grave? How can I praise you then. Can those in the grave declare your loving-kindness? Can they pro-claim your faithfulness? Can the darkness speak of your miracles? Can anyone in the Land of Forgetfulness talk about your help? O Lord, I plead for my life and will keep on pleading day by day. Psalm 88:1-13

2. I am slipping down the hill to death; I am shaken off from life as easily as a man brushes a grasshopper from his arm. My knees are weak from fasting and I am skin and bones. Help me, O Lord my God! Save me because you are loving and kind. Do it publicly, so all will see that you yourself have done it. Psalm 109:22-24, 26-27

3. Lord, hear my prayer! Listen to my plea! Don't turn away from me in this time of my distress. Bend down your ear and give me speedy answers, for my days disappear like smoke. My health is broken and my heart is sick; it is trampled like grass and is withered. My food is tasteless, and I have lost my appetite. I am reduced to skin and bones because of all my groaning and despair. I am like a vulture in a far-off wilderness, or like an owl alone in the desert. I lie awake, lonely as a solitary sparrow on the roof. Psalm 102:1-7

4. Pity me, O Lord, for I am weak. Heal me, for my body is sick, and I am upset and disturbed. My mind is filled with apprehension and with gloom. Oh, restore me soon. Come, O Lord, and make me well. In your kindness save me. I am worn out with pain; every night my pillow is wet with tears. He will answer all my prayers. Psalm 6:2-4, 6, 9

Other Prayers For Healing From The Bible

Words of encouragement

1. Dear friend, I am praying that all is well with you and that your body is as healthy as I know your soul is. 3 John 1:2

2. May God our Father and the Lord Jesus Christ give you his blessings and his peace. Philemon 1:3

3. In your day of trouble, may the Lord be with you! May the God of Jacob keep you from all harm. May he send you aid from his sanctuary in Zion. May he grant you your heart's desire and fulfill all your plans. Psalm 20:1-2, 4

4. May God our Father and the Lord Jesus Christ mightily bless each one of you, and give you peace. 2 Corinthians 1:2

5. May God bless you all. Yes, I pray that God our Father and the Lord Jesus Christ will give each of you his fullest blessings, and his peace in your hearts and your lives. And I am sure that God who began the good work within you will keep right on helping you grow in his grace until his task within you is finally finished on that day when Jesus Christ returns. Philippians 1:2, 6

6. May blessing and peace of heart be your rich gifts from God our Father, and from Jesus Christ our Lord. We always thank God for you and pray for you constantly. 1 Thessalonians 1:1b-2

7. May you be given more and more of God's kindness, peace, and love. Jude 1:2

8. Reassure me that your promises are for me, for I trust and revere you. Psalm 119:38

9. Never forget your promises to me your servant, for they are my only hope. They give me strength in all my troubles; how they refresh and revive me! Psalm 119:50-51

10. So cheer up! Take courage if you are depending on the Lord! Psalm 31:24

Prayers Of Comfort & Advice As I Wait For Healing

Words of hope

1. Be glad for all God is planning for you. Be patient in trouble, and prayerful always. Romans 12:12

2. Don't worry about anything; instead, pray about everything; tell God your needs and don't forget to thank him for his answers. If you do this you will experience God's peace, which is far more wonderful than the human mind can understand. His peace will keep your thoughts and your hearts quiet and at rest as you trust in Christ Jesus. Philippians 4:6-7

3. These troubles and sufferings of ours are, after all, quite small and won't last very long. Yet this short time of distress will result in God's rich-

est blessing upon us forever and ever! So we do not look at what we can see right now, the troubles all around us, but we look forward to the joys in heaven which we have not yet seen. The troubles will soon be over, but the joys to come will last forever. 2 Corinthians 4:17-18

4. For I am convinced that nothing can ever separate us from his love. Death can't, and life can't. The angels won't, and all the powers of hell itself cannot keep God's love away. Our fears for today, our worries about tomorrow, or where we are—high above the sky, or in the deepest ocean—nothing will ever be able to separate us from the love of God demonstrated by our Lord Jesus Christ when he died for us. Romans 8:38-39

5. We can rejoice, too, when we run into problems and trials for we know that they are good for us—they help us learn to be patient. And patience develops strength of character in us and helps us trust God more each time we use it until finally our hope and faith are strong and steady. Then, when that happens, we are able to hold our heads high no matter what happens and know that all is well, for we know how dearly God loves us, and we feel this warm love everywhere within us because God

has given us the Holy Spirit to fill our hearts with his love. Romans 5:3-5

6. For examples of patience in suffering, look at the Lord's prophets. We know how happy they are now because they stayed true to him then, even though they suffered greatly for it. Job is an example of a man who continued to trust the Lord in sorrow; from his experiences we can see how the Lord's plan finally ended in good, for he is full of tenderness and mercy. James 5:10-11

Prayers Of Thanksgiving And Praise For God's Healing In My Life

I can thank the Lord who has saved me

1. Say "Thank You" to the Lord for being so good, for always being so loving and kind. Psalm 107:1

2. He asked for a long, good life, and you have granted his request; the days of his life stretch on and on forever. Psalm 21:4

3. All heaven shall praise your miracles, O Lord; myriads of angels will praise you for your faithfulness. Psalm 89:5

4. I lie awake at night thinking of you—of how much you have helped me—and how I rejoice through the night beneath the protecting shad-

ow of your wings. I follow close behind you, protected by your strong right arm. Psalm 63:6-8

5. But as for me, I will sing each morning about your power and mercy. For you have been my high tower of refuge, a place of safety in the day of my distress. O my Strength, to you I sing my praises; for you are my high tower of safety, my God of mercy. Psalm 59:16-17

6. We live within the shadow of the Almighty, sheltered by the God who is above all gods. This I declare, that he alone is my refuge, my place of safety; he is my God, and I am trusting him. For he rescues you from every trap, and protects you from the fatal plague. He will shield you with his wings! They will shelter you. His faithful promises are your armor. Now you don't need to be afraid of the dark any more, nor fear the dangers of the day; nor dread the plagues of darkness, nor disasters in the morning. Psalm 91:1-6

I can offer praise to God for his deeds of power and healing

1. Thank you, Lord! How good you are! Your love for us continues on forever. Who can ever list

the glorious miracles of God? Who can ever praise him half enough? Psalm 106:1b-2

2. How we thank you, Lord! Your mighty miracles give proof that you care. Psalm 75:1

3. All the earth shall worship you and sing of your glories. Come, see the glorious things God has done. What marvelous miracles happen to his people! Psalm 66:4-5

4. O Lord my God, many and many a time you have done great miracles for us, and we are ever in your thoughts. Who else can do such glorious things? No one else can be compared with you. There isn't time to tell of all your wonderful deeds. Psalm 40:5

5. I recall the many miracles he did for me so long ago. Those wonderful deeds are constantly in my thoughts. I cannot stop thinking about them. Psalm 77:11-12

6. You are the God of miracles and wonders! You still demonstrate your awesome power. Psalm 77:14

7. I will reveal these truths to you so that you can describe these glorious deeds of Jehovah to your children, and tell them about the mighty miracles he did. For he gave his laws to Israel, and commanded our fathers to teach them to

their children, so that they in turn could teach their children too. Thus his laws pass down from generation to generation. In this way each generation has been able to obey his laws and to set its hope anew on God and not forget his glorious miracles. Psalm 78:4-7

8. O Lord, what miracles you do! And how deep are your thoughts! Psalm 92:5

CHAPTER THREE

Accounts Of God's Healing From The Bible

Key Verse:

In solemn truth I tell you, anyone believing in me shall do the same miracles I have done, and even greater ones, because I am going to be with the Father. You can ask him for anything, using my name, and I will do it, for this will bring praise to the Father because of what I, the Son, will do for you. Yes, ask anything, using my name, and I will do it! John 14:12-14

Christ's Healing Miracles

Jesus heals because of his compassion

1. While in Capernaum Jesus went over to the synagogue again, and noticed a man there with a deformed hand. Since it was the Sabbath, Jesus' enemies watched him closely. Would he heal the man's hand? If he did, they planned to arrest him! Jesus asked the man to come and stand in front of the congregation. Then turning to his enemies he asked, "Is it all right to do kind deeds on Sabbath days? Or is this a day for doing harm? Is it a day to save lives or to destroy them?" But they wouldn't answer him. Looking around at them angrily, for he was deeply disturbed by their indifference to human need, he said to the man, "Reach out your hand." He did, and instantly his hand was healed! Mark 3:1-5 (See also the same account in Matthew 12:9-13 and Luke 6:6-10)

2. Then, leaving the synagogue, he and his disciples went over to Simon and Andrew's home, where they found Simon's mother-in-law sick in bed with a high fever. They told Jesus about her right away. He went to her bedside, and as he took her by the hand and helped her to sit up, the fever suddenly left, and she got up and prepared dinner for them! By sunset the courtyard was filled with the sick and demon-possessed, brought to him for healing; and a huge crowd of people from all over the city of Capernaum gathered outside the door to watch. So Jesus healed great numbers of sick folk that evening and ordered many demons to come out of their victims. (But he refused to allow the demons to speak, because they knew who he was.) Mark 1:29-34 (See also the same account in Matthew 8:14-17 and Luke 4:38-41)

3. One Sabbath as he was in the home of a member of the Jewish Council, the Pharisees were watching him like hawks to see if he would heal a man who was present who was suffering from dropsy. Jesus said to the Pharisees and legal experts standing round, "Well, is it within the Law to heal a man on the Sabbath day, or not?" And when they refused to answer, Jesus took the sick man by the hand and healed him

47

and sent him away. Then he turned to them; "Which of you doesn't work on the Sabbath?" he asked. "If your cow falls into a pit, don't you proceed at once to get it out?" Again they had no answer. Luke 14:1-6

4. One Sabbath as he was teaching in a synagogue, he saw a seriously handicapped woman who had been bent double for eighteen years and was unable to straighten herself. Calling her over to him Jesus said, "Woman, you are healed of your sickness!" He touched her, and instantly she could stand straight. How she praised and thanked God! Luke 13:10-13

5. Leaving that place, Jesus met a man who couldn't speak because a demon was inside him. So Jesus cast out the demon, and instantly the man could talk. How the crowds marveled! "Never in all our lives have we seen anything like this," they exclaimed. Matthew 9:32-33

6. But Jesus said, "Judas, how can you do this— betray the Messiah with a kiss?" When the other disciples saw what was about to happen, they exclaimed, "Master, shall we fight? We brought along the swords!" And one of them slashed at the High Priest's servant and cut off his right ear. But Jesus said, "Don't resist any more." And he touched the place where the

man's ear had been and restored it. Luke
22:48-51

7. So when Jesus came out of the wilderness, a
vast crowd was waiting for him and he pitied
them and healed their sick. Matthew 14:14

Jesus heals because of their faith

1. As Jesus was leaving his home, two blind men
followed along behind, shouting, "O Son of
King David, have mercy on us." They went
right into the house where he was staying, and
Jesus asked them, "Do you believe I can make
you see?" "Yes, Lord," they told him, "we do."
Then he touched their eyes and said, "Because
of your faith it will happen." And suddenly they
could see! Matthew 9:27-30a

2. One day in a certain village he was visiting,
there was a man with an advanced case of leprosy. When he saw Jesus he fell to the ground
before him, face downward in the dust, begging to be healed. "Sir," he said, "if you only
will, you can clear me of every trace of my disease." Jesus reached out and touched the man
and said, "Of course I will. Be healed." And the
leprosy left him instantly! Then Jesus instruct-
ed him to go at once without telling anyone

49

what had happened and be examined by the Jewish priest. "Offer the sacrifice Moses' law requires for lepers who are healed," he said. "This will prove to everyone that you are well." Now the report of his power spread even faster and vast crowds came to hear him preach and to be healed of their diseases. Luke 5:12-15 (See also the same account in Matthew 8:2-4 and Mark 1:40-44.)

3. In the crowd was a woman who had been sick for twelve years with a hemorrhage. She had suffered much from many doctors through the years and had become poor from paying them, and was no better but, in fact, was worse. She had heard all about the wonderful miracles Jesus did, and that is why she came up behind him through the crowd and touched his clothes. For she thought to herself, "If I can just touch his clothing, I will be healed." And sure enough, as soon as she had touched him, the bleeding stopped and she knew she was well! Jesus realized at once that healing power had gone out from him, so he turned around in the crowd and asked, "Who touched my clothes?" His disciples said to him, "All this crowd pressing around you, and you ask who touched you?" But he kept on looking around

to see who it was who had done it. Then the frightened woman, trembling at the realization of what had happened to her, came and fell at his feet and told him what she had done. And he said to her, "Daughter, your faith has made you well; go in peace, healed of your disease." Mark 5:25-34 (See also the same account in Matthew 9:20-22 and Luke 8:43-48.)

4. And so they reached Jericho. Later, as they left town, a great crowd was following. Now it happened that a blind beggar named Bartimaeus (the son of Timaeus) was sitting beside the road as Jesus was going by. When Bartimaeus heard that Jesus from Nazareth was near, he began to should out, "Jesus, Son of David, have mercy on me!" "Shut up!" some of the people yelled at him. But he only shouted the louder, again and again, "O Son of David, have mercy on me!" When Jesus heard him he stopped there in the road and said, "Tell him to come here." So they called the blind man. "You lucky fellow," they said, "come on, he's calling you!" Bartimaeus yanked off his old coat and flung it aside, jumped up and came to Jesus. "What do you want me to do for you?" Jesus asked. "O Teacher," the blind man said, "I want to see!" And Jesus said to him, "All right, it's done. Your

faith has healed you." And instantly the blind man could see, and followed Jesus down the road! Mark 10:46-52 (See also the same account in Luke 18:35-43 and a similar one in Matthew 20:30-34.)

5. As they continued onward toward Jerusalem, they reached the border between Galilee and Samaria, and as they entered a village there, ten lepers stood at the distance, crying out, "Jesus, sir, have mercy on us!" He looked at them and said, "Go to the Jewish priest and show him that you are healed!" And as they were going, their leprosy disappeared. One of them came back to Jesus, shouting, "Glory to God, I'm healed!" He fell flat on the ground in front of Jesus, face downward in the dust, thanking him for what he had done. This man was a despised Samaritan. Jesus asked, "Didn't I heal ten men? Where are the nine? Does only this foreigner return to give glory to God?" And Jesus said to the man, "Stand up and go; your faith has made you well." Luke 17:11-19

Jesus heals because of the faith of others

1. A deaf man with a speech impediment was brought to him, and everyone begged Jesus to lay his hands on the man and heal him. Jesus led him away from the crowd and put his fingers into the man's ears, then spat and touched the man's tongue with the spittle. Then, looking up to heaven, he sighed and commanded, "Open!" Instantly the man could hear perfectly and speak plainly! Mark 7:32-35

2. When they arrived at Bethsaida, some people brought a blind man to him and begged him to touch and heal him. Jesus took the blind man by the hand and led him out of the village, and spat upon his eyes, and laid his hands over them. "Can you see anything now?" Jesus asked him. The man looked around. "Yes!" he said, "I see men! But I can't see them very clearly; they look like tree trunks walking around!" Then Jesus placed his hands over the man's eyes again and as the man stared intently, his sight was completely restored, and he saw everything clearly, drinking in the sights around him. Mark 8:22-25

3. Several days later he returned to Capernaum, and the news of his arrival spread quickly through the city. Four men arrived carrying a paralyzed man on a stretcher. They couldn't get to Jesus through the crowd, so they dug

through the clay roof above his head and lowered the sick man on his stretcher, right down in front of Jesus. When Jesus saw how strongly they believed that he would help, Jesus said to the sick man, "Son, your sins are forgiven!...I, the Messiah, have the authority on earth to forgive sins. But talk is cheap—anybody could say that. So I'll prove it to you by healing this man." Then, turning to the paralyzed man, he commanded, "Pick up your stretcher and go on home, for you are healed!" The man jumped up, took the stretcher, and pushed his way through the stunned onlookers! Then how they praised God. "We've never seen anything like this before!" they all exclaimed. Mark 2:1, 3-5, 9-12 (See also the same account in Luke 5:17-26 and Matthew 9:1-8.)

4. When Jesus arrived in Capernaum, a Roman army captain came and pled with him to come to his home and heal his servant boy who was in bed paralyzed and racked with pain. "Yes," Jesus said, "I will come and heal him." Then the officer said, "Sir, I am not worthy to have you in my home; [and it isn't necessary for you to come]. If you will only stand here and say, 'Be healed,' my servant will get well! I know, because I am under

the authority of my superior officers and I have authority over my soldiers, and I say to one, 'Go,' and he goes, and to another, 'Come,' and he comes, and to my slave boy, 'Do this or that,' and he does it. And I know you have authority to tell his sickness to go—and it will go!" Jesus stood there amazed! Turning to the crowd he said, "I haven't seen faith like this in all the land of Israel! And I tell you this, that many Gentiles [like this Roman officer], shall come from all over the world and sit down in the Kingdom of Heaven with Abraham, Isaac, and Jacob. And many an Israelite—those for whom the Kingdom was prepared—shall be cast into outer darkness, into the place of weeping and torment." Then Jesus said to the Roman officer, "Go on home. What you have believed has happened!" And the boy was healed that same hour! Matthew 8:5-13 (See also the same account in Luke 7:1-10.)

5. Then a demon-possessed man—he was both blind and unable to talk—was brought to Jesus, and Jesus healed him so that he could both speak and see. The crowd was amazed. "Maybe Jesus is the Messiah!" they exclaimed. Matthew 12:22-23

1. In the course of his journey through Galilee he arrived at the town of Cana, where he had turned the water into wine. While he was there, a man in the city of Capernaum, a government official, whose son was very sick, heard that Jesus had come from Judea and was traveling in Galilee. This man went over to Cana, found Jesus, and begged him to come to Capernaum with him and heal his son, who was now at death's door. Jesus asked, "Won't any of you believe in me unless I do more and more miracles?" The official pled, "Sir, please come now before my child dies." Then Jesus told him, "Go back home. Your son is healed!" And the man believed Jesus and started home. While he was on his way, some of his servants met him with the news that all was well—his son had recovered. He asked them when the lad had begun to feel better, and they replied, "Yesterday afternoon at about one o'clock his fever suddenly disappeared!" Then the father realized it was the same moment that Jesus had told him, "Your son is healed." And the officer and his entire household believed that Jesus was the Messiah. John 4:46-53

2. A woman from Canaan who was living there

came to him, pleading, "Have mercy on me, O Lord, King David's Son! For my daughter has a demon within her, and it torments her constantly." But Jesus gave her no reply—not even a word. Then his disciples urged him to send her away. "Tell her to get going," they said, "for she is bothering us with all her begging." But she came and worshiped him and pled again, "Sir, help me!" "It doesn't seem right to take bread from the children and throw it to the dogs," he said. "Yes, it is!" she replied, "for even the puppies beneath the table are permitted to eat the crumbs that fall." "Woman," Jesus told her, "your faith is large, and your request is granted." And her daughter was healed right then. Matthew 15:22-28 (See also the same account in Mark 7:25-30.)

Jesus heals to bring glory to the Father

1. Inside the city, near the Sheep Gate, was Bethesda Pool, with five covered platforms or porches surrounding it. Crowds of sick folks— lame, blind, or with paralyzed limbs—lay on the platforms (waiting for a certain movement of the water, for an angel of the Lord came from time to time and disturbed the water, and the first person to step down into it afterwards

was healed.) One of the men lying there had been sick for thirty-eight years. When Jesus saw him and knew how long he had been ill, he asked him, "Would you like to get well?" "I can't," the sick man said, "for I have no one to help me into the pool at the movement of the water. While I am trying to get there, someone else always gets in ahead of me." Jesus told him, "Stand up, roll up your sleeping mat and go on home!" Instantly, the man was healed! He rolled up the mat and began walking! John 5:2-9a

2. As he was walking along, he saw a man blind from birth. "Master," his disciples asked him, "why was this man born blind? Was it a result of his own sins or those of his parents?" "Neither," Jesus answered. "But to demonstrate the power of God. All of us must quickly carry out the tasks assigned us by the one who sent me, for there is little time left before the night falls and all work comes to an end. But while I am still here in the world, I give it my light." Then he spat on the ground and made mud from the spittle and smoothed the mud over the blind man's eyes, and told him, "Go and wash in the Pool of Siloam" (the word "Siloam" means "Sent"). So the man went where he was sent and washed and came back seeing! His neighbors and others who knew him as a blind beggar asked each other, "Is this the same fellow—that beggar?" Some said yes, and some said no. "It can't be the same man," they thought, "but he surely looks like him!" And the beggar said, "I am the same man!" Then they asked him how in the world he could see. What had happened? And he told them, "A man they call Jesus made mud and smoothed it over my eyes and told me to go to the Pool of Siloam and wash off the mud. I did, and I can see!" John 9:1-11 (Read the rest of this account in John 9:12-41.)

3. Once as he was teaching in the synagogue, a man possessed by a demon began shouting at Jesus, "Go away!" We want nothing to do with you, Jesus from Nazareth. You have come to destroy us. I know who you are—the Holy Son of God." Jesus cut him short. "Be silent!" he told the demon. "Come out!" The demon threw the man to the floor as the crowd watched, and then left him without hurting him further. Amazed, the people asked, "What is in this man's words that even demons obey him?" Luke 4:33-36 (See also the same account in Mark 1:23-27.)

4. One of the men in the crowd spoke up and said, "Teacher, I brought my son for you to heal—he can't talk because he is possessed by a demon. And whenever the demon is in control of him it dashes him to the ground and makes him foam at the mouth and grind his teeth and become rigid. So I begged your disciples to cast out the demon, but they couldn't do it." Jesus said [to his disciples], "Oh, what tiny faith you have; how much longer must I be with you until you believe? How much longer must I be patient with you? Bring the boy to me." So they brought the boy, but when he saw Jesus the demon convulsed the child horribly, and he fell to the ground writhing and foaming at the mouth. "How long has he been this way?" Jesus asked the father. And he replied, "Since he was very small, and the demon often makes him fall into the fire or into water to kill him. Oh, have mercy on us and do something if you can." "If I can?" Jesus asked. "Anything is possible if you have faith." The father instantly replied, "I do have faith; oh, help me to have more!" When Jesus saw the crowd growing he rebuked the demon. "O demon of deafness and dumbness," he said, "I command you to come out of this child and enter him no more!" Then the demon screamed terribly and convulsed the boy again and left him; and the boy lay there limp and motionless, to all appearance dead. A murmur ran through the crowd—"He is dead." But Jesus took him by the hand and helped him to his feet and he stood up and was all right! Afterwards, when Jesus was alone in the house with his disciples, they asked him, "Why couldn't we cast that demon out?" Jesus replied, "Cases like this require prayer." Mark 9:17-29 (See also the same account in Matthew 17:14-21 and Luke 9:37-43.)

5. When they arrived at the other side of the lake a demon-possessed man ran out from a graveyard, just as Jesus was climbing from the boat. This man lived among the gravestones, and had such strength that whenever he was put into handcuffs and shackles—as he often was—he snapped the handcuffs from his wrists and smashed the shackles and walked away. No one was strong enough to control him. All day long and through the night he would wander among the tombs and in the wild hills, screaming and cutting himself with sharp pieces of stone. When Jesus was still far out on the water, the man had seen him and had run to meet him, and fell down before him. Then

Jesus spoke to the demon within the man and said, "Come out, you evil spirit." It gave a terrible scream, shrieking, "What are you going to do to me, Jesus, Son of the Most High God? For God's sake, don't torture me!" "What is your name?" Jesus asked, and the demon replied, "Legion, for there are many of us here within this man." Then the demons begged him again and again not to send them to some distant land. Now as it happened there was a huge herd of hogs rooting around on the hill above the lake. "Send us into those hogs," the demons begged. And Jesus gave them permission. Then the evil spirits came out of the man and entered the hogs, and the entire herd plunged down the steep hillside into the lake and drowned. The herdsmen fled to the nearby towns and countryside, spreading the news as they ran. Everyone rushed out to see for themselves. And a large crowd soon gathered where Jesus was; but as they saw the man sitting there, fully clothed and perfectly sane, they were frightened. Those who saw what happened were telling everyone about it, and the crowd began pleading with Jesus to go away and leave them alone! The man who had been possessed by the demons begged Jesus to let him go along. But Jesus said no. "Go home to your friends," he told him, "and tell them what wonderful things God has done for you; and how merciful he has been. So the man started off to visit the Ten Towns of that region and began to tell everyone about the great things Jesus had done for him; and they were awestruck by his story. Mark 5:1-20 (See also the same account in Luke 8:26-39 and Matthew 8:28-34.)

Other testimonies of Jesus' healings

1. Jesus' disciples saw him do many other miracles besides the ones told about in this book, but these are recorded so that you will believe that he is the Messiah, the Son of God, and that believing in him you will have life. John 20:30-31

2. That evening several demon-possessed people were brought to Jesus; and when he spoke a single word, all the demons fled; and all the sick were healed. This fulfilled the prophecy of Isaiah, "He took our sicknesses and bore our diseases." Matthew 8:16-17

3. Jesus traveled around through all the cities and villages of that area, teaching in the Jewish

synagogues and announcing the Good News about the Kingdom. And wherever he went he healed people of every sort of illness. And what pity he felt for the crowds that came, because their problems were so great and they didn't know what to do or where to go for help. They were like sheep without a shepherd. Matthew 9:35-36

4. And a vast crowd brought him their lame, blind, maimed, and those who couldn't speak, and many others, and laid them before Jesus, and he healed them all. What a spectacle it was! Those who hadn't been able to say a word before were talking excitedly, and those with missing arms and legs had new ones; the crippled were walking and jumping around, and those who had been blind were gazing about them! The crowds just marveled, and praised the God of Israel. Matthew 15:30-31 (See also Mark 6:53-56.)

5. As the sun went down that evening, all the villagers who had any sick people in their homes, no matter what their diseases were, brought them to Jesus; and the touch of his hands healed every one! Luke 4:40

6. But the crowds found out where he was going,

and followed. And he welcomed them, teaching them again about the Kingdom of God and curing those who were ill. Luke 9:11

7. Jesus traveled all through Galilee teaching in the Jewish synagogues, everywhere preaching the Good News about the Kingdom of Heaven. And he healed every kind of sickness and disease. The report of his miracles spread far beyond the borders of Galilee so that sick folk were soon coming from as far away as Syria. And whatever their illness and pain, or if they were possessed by demons, or were insane, or paralyzed—he healed them all. Matthew 4:23-24

8. He healed the sick among them, but he cautioned them against spreading the news about his miracles. Matthew 12:15b-16

9. They landed at Gennesaret. The news of their arrival spread quickly throughout the city, and soon people were rushing around, telling everyone to bring in their sick to be healed. The sick begged him to let them touch even the tassel of his robe, and all who did were healed. Matthew 14:34-36

10. Vast crowds followed him, and he healed their sick. Matthew 19:2

11. And now the blind and crippled came to him and he healed them in the Temple. Matthew 21:14

12. For there had been many healings that day and as a result great numbers of sick people were crowding around him, trying to touch him. Mark 3:10

13. And because of their unbelief he couldn't do any mighty miracles among them except to place his hands on a few sick people and heal them. And he could hardly accept the fact that they wouldn't believe in him. Mark 6:5-6

14. When they came down the slopes of the mountain, they stood with Jesus on a large, level area, surrounded by many of his followers who, in turn, were surrounded by the crowds. For people from all over Judea and from Jerusalem and from as far north as the sea-coasts of Tyre and Sidon had come to hear him or to be healed. And he cast out many demons. Everyone was trying to touch him, for when they did healing power went out from him and they were cured. Luke 6:17-19

15. And a huge crowd, many of them pilgrims on their way to Jerusalem for the annual Passover celebration, were following him wherever he went, to watch him heal the sick. John 6:2

16. And you no doubt know that Jesus of Nazareth was anointed by God with the Holy Spirit and with power, and he went around doing good and healing all who were possessed by demons, for God was with him. Acts 10:38

The Disciples' Healing Miracles

Peter heals the sick

1. Peter and John went to the Temple one afternoon to take part in the three o'clock daily prayer meeting. As they approached the Temple, they saw a man lame from birth carried along the street and laid beside the Temple gate—the one called The Beautiful Gate—as was his custom every day. As Peter and John were passing by, he asked them for some money. They looked at him intently, and then Peter said, "Look here!" The lame man looked at them eagerly, expecting a gift. But Peter said, "We don't have any money for you! But I'll give you something else! I command you in the name of Jesus Christ of Nazareth, walk!" Then Peter took the lame man by the hand and pulled him to his feet. And as he did, the man's feet and ankle-bones were healed and strengthened so that he came up with a leap, stood there a moment and began walking! Then, walking, leaping, and praising God, he went into the Temple with them...Peter saw his opportunity and addressed the crowd..."Jesus' name has healed this man—and you know how lame he was before. Faith in Jesus' name—faith given us from God—has caused this perfect healing." Acts 3:1-8, 12a, 16

2. Sick people were brought out into the streets on beds and mats so that at least Peter's shadow would fall across some of them as he went by! And crowds came in from the Jerusalem suburbs, bringing their sick folk and those possessed by demons; and every one of them was healed. Acts 5:15-16

3. Peter traveled from place to place to visit them, and in his travels came to the believers in the town of Lydda. There he met a man named Aeneas, paralyzed and bed-ridden for eight years. Peter said to him, "Aeneas! Jesus Christ has healed you! Get up and make your bed." And he was healed instantly. Acts 9:32-34

Philip heals the sick

1. Philip, for instance, went to the city of Samaria and told the people there about Christ. Crowds listened intently to what he had to say because of the miracles he did. Many evil spirits were cast out, screaming as they left their victims, and many who were paralyzed or lame were healed. Acts 8:5-7

Paul heals the sick

1. While they were at Lystra, they came upon a man with crippled feet who had been that way from birth, so he had never walked. He was listening as Paul preached, and Paul noticed him and realized he had faith to be healed. So Paul called to him, "Stand up!" and the man leaped to his feet and started walking! Acts 14:8-10

2. And God gave Paul the power to do unusual miracles, so that even when his handkerchiefs or parts of his clothing were placed upon sick people, they were healed, and any demons within them came out. Acts 19:11-12

3. As it happened, Publius' father was ill with fever and dysentery. Paul went in and prayed for him, and laying his hands on him, healed him! Then all the other sick people in the island came and were cured. Acts 28:8-9

4. One day as we were going down to the place of prayer beside the river, we met a demon-possessed slave girl who was a fortune-teller, and earned much money for her masters. She followed along behind us shouting, "These men are servants of God and they have come to tell you how to have your sins forgiven." This went on day after day until Paul, in great distress, turned and spoke to the demon within her. "I command you in the name of Jesus Christ to come out of her," he said. And instantly it left her. Acts 16:16-18

Other testimonies to the disciples' healings

1. So they began their circuit of the villages, preaching the Good News and healing the sick. Luke 9:6

2. So the disciples went out, telling everyone they met to turn from sin. And they cast out many demons, and healed many sick people, anointing them with olive oil. Mark 6:12-13

3. Meanwhile, the apostles were meeting regularly at the Temple in the area known as

Solomon's Hall, and they did many remarkable miracles among the people. Acts 5:12

4. So Ananias went over and found Paul and laid his hands on him and said, "Brother Paul, the Lord Jesus, who appeared to you on the road, has sent me so that you may be filled with the Holy Spirit and get your sight back." Instantly (it was as though scales fell from his eyes) Paul could see, and was immediately baptized. Acts 9:17-19a

Jesus promises his followers the authority and power to heal

1. Jesus called his twelve disciples to him, and gave them authority to cast out evil spirits and to heal every kind of sickness and disease...Jesus sent them out with these instructions: "...Heal the sick, raise the dead, cure the lepers, and cast out demons. Give as freely as you have received!" Matthew 10:1, 5a, 8

2. And those who believe shall use my authority to cast out demons, and they shall speak new languages. They will be able even to handle snakes with safety, and if they drink anything poisonous, it won't hurt them; and they will be able to place their hands on the sick and heal them. Mark 16:17-18

3. If a town welcomes you, follow these two rules: (1) Eat whatever is set before you. (2) Heal the sick; and as you heal them, say, "The Kingdom of God is very near you now." Luke 10:8-9

4. After the apostles returned to Jesus and report- ed what they had done, he slipped quietly away with them toward the city of Bethsaida. But the crowds found out where he was going, and followed. And he welcomed them, teaching them again about the Kingdom of God and curing those who were ill. Luke 9:10-11

5. He gives special faith to another, and to someone else the power to heal the sick. 1 Corinthians 12:9

Other testimonies of God's healing

1. I cried out to the Lord, and he heard me from his Temple in Jerusalem. Then I lay down and slept in peace and woke up safely, for the Lord was watching over me. Psalm 3:4-5

2. Then they cried to the Lord in their troubles, and he helped them and delivered them. He spoke, and they were healed—snatched from the door of death. Psalm 107:19-20

3. In my distress I prayed to the Lord and he answered me and rescued me. He is for me! How can I be afraid? What can mere man do to me? Psalm 118:5-6

4. In my troubles I pled with God to help me and he did! Psalm 120:1

5. But after that time Hezekiah became deathly sick, and he prayed to the Lord, and the Lord replied with a miracle. 2 Chronicles 32:24

6. I love the Lord because he hears my prayers and answers them. Because he bends down and listens, I will pray as long as I breathe! Death stared me in the face—I was frightened and sad. Then I cried, "Lord, save me!" How kind he is! How good he is! So merciful, this God of ours! The Lord protects the simple and childlike; I was facing death and then he saved me. Now I can relax. For the Lord has done this wonderful miracle for me. He has saved me from death, my eyes from tears, my feet from stumbling. I shall live! Yes, in his presence—here on earth! In my discouragement I thought, "They are lying when they say I will recover." But now what can I offer Jehovah for all he has done for me? I will bring him an offering of wine and praise his name for saving me. I will publicly bring him the sacrifice I vowed I would. His loved ones are very precious to him and he vows not lightly let them die. O Lord, you have freed me from my bonds and I will serve you forever. I will worship you and offer you a sacrifice of thanksgiving. Psalm 116:1-17

7. It was just before all this that Hezekiah became deathly sick and Isaiah the prophet (Amoz' son) went to visit him and gave him this message from the Lord: "Set your affairs in order, for you are going to die; you will not recover from this illness." When Hezekiah heard this, he turned his face to the wall and prayed: "O Lord, don't you remember how true I've been to you and how I've always tried to obey you in everything you said?" Then he broke down with great sobs. So the Lord sent another message to Isaiah: "Go and tell Hezekiah that the Lord God of your forefather David hears you praying and sees your tears and will let you live fifteen more years. He will deliver you and this city from the king of Assyria. I will defend you, says the Lord, and here is my guarantee: I will send the sun backwards ten degrees as measured on Ahaz sun dial!" So the sun retraced ten degrees that it had gone down! When King Hezekiah was well again, he wrote this poem about his experience: "My life is but half done

and I must leave it all. I am robbed of my normal years, and now I must enter the gates of Sheol. Never again will I see the Lord in the land of the living. Never again will I see my friends in this world. My life is blown away like a shepherd's tent; it is cut short as when a weaver stops his working at the loom. In one short day my life hangs by a thread. All night I moaned; it was like being torn apart by lions. Delirious, I chattered like a swallow and mourned like a dove; my eyes grew weary of looking up for help. 'O God,' I cried, 'I am in trouble—help me.' But what can I say? For he himself has sent this sickness. All my sleep has fled because of my soul's bitterness. O Lord, your discipline is good and leads to life and health. Oh, heal me and make me live! Yes, now I see it all—it was good for me to undergo this bitterness, for you have lovingly delivered me from death; you have forgiven all my sins. For dead men cannot praise you. They cannot be filled with hope and joy. The living, only the living, can praise you as I do today. One generation makes known your faithfulness to the next. Think of it! The Lord healed me! Every day of my life from now on I will sing my songs of praise in the Temple, accompanied by the orchestra." Isaiah 38:1-20

$\mathscr{P}$rayers For My Healing

(paraphrased from The Book of Common Prayer of the
Episcopal Church)

Key Verse:
And we are sure of this, that he will listen to us
whenever we ask him for anything in line with his
will. And if we really know he is listening when we
talk to him and make our requests, then we can be
sure that he will answer us. 1 John 5:14-15

For my recovery from illness

1. O Father of mercies and God of all comfort, my only help in this time of need; I humbly beg you to visit me and take away my sickness. Look upon me with the eyes of your mercy; comfort me with a sense of your love; preserve me from the temptations of the enemy; and give me patience under my affliction. In your good time, restore me to health and enable me to lead the rest of my life to your glory. Grant that finally I may dwell with you in life everlasting, through Jesus Christ my Lord. Amen.

2. Dear Jesus, the source of all health: Fill my heart with faith in your love so that with calm expectancy I may make room for your power and gracefully accept your healing. Amen.

3. Jesus, be with me in this time of crisis in my life. For the glory of your Name, turn from me all those evils I have most justly deserved. Grant that in all my troubles I may continually put my whole trust and confidence in your mercy and power to save, heal, and restore. Amen.

When I am in pain

Lord Jesus Christ, by your patience in suffering

you hallowed earthly pain and gave me the example of obedience to my Father's will. Be near me in my time of weakness and pain; sustain me by your grace, that my strength and courage may not fail; heal me according to your will; and help me always to believe that what happens to the earthly me is of little account if you hold me in eternal life, my Lord and my God. Amen.

Before my operation

Strengthen me, O Lord, to do what I have to do and bear what I have to bear; that by accepting your healing gifts through the skill of surgeons and nurses, I may be restored to health with a thankful heart. Amen.

For my doctors and nurses

O Lord, sanctify those whom you have called to the practice of the arts of healing and to the prevention of disease and pain. Strengthen them by your life-giving Spirit, that by their ministries my health may be renewed and your creation glorified. Amen.

For the sanctification of my illness

Sanctify my illness, O Lord, that the sense of my weakness may add strength to my faith and seriousness to my repentance. Grant that I may live with you in life everlasting when Jesus calls me home. Amen.

For the healing power of sleep

O heavenly Father, you give your children sleep to refresh soul and body. Grant me this gift, I pray; keep me in that perfect peace which you have promised to those whose minds are fixed on you. Give me such a sense of your presence that in the hours of silence I may enjoy the blessed assurance of your love, through Jesus Christ my Lord. Amen.

For strength at the beginning of each new day

Dear Lord, this is another day. Make me ready, Lord, for whatever it may bring. If I am to stand up, help me to stand bravely. If I am to sit still, help me to sit quietly. If I am to lie low, help me to do it patiently. And if I am to do nothing, let me do it gallantly. May these words be more than words—give me the power and the Spirit of Jesus. Amen.

A thanksgiving when I begin to recover

Jesus, your compassion never fails and your mercies are new every morning. I give you thanks for giving me both relief from pain and hope of renewed health. Continue in me, I pray, the good work you have begun; that daily increasing in bodily strength, and rejoicing in your goodness, I may so order my life and conduct that I may always think and do those things that please and glorify you. Amen.

For the forgiveness and healing of my sins

1. Almighty and everlasting God, you hate nothing you have made and forgive the sins of all who are penitent. Create in me a new and contrite heart, that I, worthily lamenting my sins and acknowledging my wretchedness, may obtain of you, the God of all mercy, perfect remission and forgiveness, through Jesus Christ my Lord. Amen.

2. Dear Father in heaven, you are always more ready to hear than I am to pray and willing to give more than I either desire or deserve: Pour upon me the abundance of your mercy, healing me of those things which trouble my conscience and giving me those good things for which I am not worthy to ask, except through the merits and mediation of Jesus Christ my Lord. Amen.

For the healing of my fears and doubts

1. Most loving Father, whose will it is for me to give thanks for all things, to fear nothing but the loss of you, and to cast all my care on you who cares for me: Heal me of my faithless fears and worldly anxieties, that no clouds of this mortal life may hide from me the light of your love which is immortal and manifested in your Son Jesus Christ. Amen.

2. O Heavenly Father, have mercy upon me in my confusion and mental darkness. Restore to me strength of mind and cheerful spirit, and give me health and peace through the healing power of Jesus. Amen.

3. My Father in heaven, who guides the meek and gives light to the godly living in a world of darkness: Grant me, in all my doubts and uncertainties, the grace to ask what you would have me do. Save me from false choices by your Spirit of wisdom, and let me see life in your light so I may not stumble on your straight path. Lord, guide me always by the hand of Jesus. Amen.

For the healing of my sorrow

Grant to me, O Lord, the spirit of faith and

courage, that I may have strength to meet the days to come with steadfastness and patience—not sorrowing as those without hope, but in thankful remembrance of your great goodness, and in joyful expectation of eternal life with those I love. This I ask in the Name of Jesus who died and rose from the dead that those who believe in him might live forever. Amen.

For the healing of my addiction

O blessed Lord, you ministered to all who came to you: Look upon me with compassion in my addiction as I have lost my health and freedom. Restore to me the assurance of your unfailing mercy; remove the fears that beset my mind; strengthen me in my recovery; give patient understanding and persevering love to those who care for me; and by the power of your indwelling Spirit heal me in the days to come. Amen.

For the healing of my marriage

Jesus my Lord, send the power of your reconciling love and help us restore our relationship in you. Grant us wisdom and devotion in the ordering of our common life, that we may once again be to each other a strength in need, a counselor in perplexity, a comfort in sorrow, and a companion in joy. Knit together our wills in your will and our spirits in your Spirit so we may live together in peace in the days to come. Amen.

When death is near

1. O Father of mercies and God of all comfort, my only help in time of need: I fly to you for help as I lie here in great weakness of body. Look graciously upon me, O Lord, and as my outward body decays, strengthen me continually with your grace and Holy Spirit in my inner being. Give me unfeigned repentance for all the errors of my past and steadfast faith in your Son Jesus; that my sins may be forgiven by your mercy and my pardon sealed in heaven. This I pray in the Name of Jesus. Amen.

2. Lord Jesus Christ, by your death you took away the sting of death. Grant that I may follow in faith where you have led the way, that I may someday fall asleep peacefully in you and wake up in your likeness. Amen.

My Personal Journey of Healing

(Notes, Prayers, and Experiences)

_____

_____

_____

_____

_____

_____

_____

_____

_____